JAGGED ROCKS OF
WISDOM

OTHER BOOKS FROM
THE FINE PRINT PRESS

Jagged Rocks of Wisdom

Professional Advice for the New Attorney

Morten Lund

The Fine Print Press
Honolulu

The Fine Print Press, Ltd.
Honolulu, Hawaii
Website: www.fineprintpress.com
Email: info@fineprintpress.com

ISBN: 1-888960-07-8
ISBN: 978-1-888960-07-5
LCCN: 2006941045

Publisher's Cataloging-in-Publication Data
Lund, Morten
    Jagged Rocks of Wisdom: Professional Advice for the New Attorney
    Includes index.
        1. Law Practice   2. Legal Profession
    3. Lawyers—Practical Guides

Cover design by Jim Oertle, Designwoerks, Wichita, Kansas
Typesetting by Darleen Oertle, Designwoerks, Wichita, Kansas

Printed in the United States of America
15 14 13 12 11 10 09 08   10 9 8 7 6 5 4 3 2

CONTENTS

Acknowledgements

Thanks are due to the partners at Foley & Lardner LLP, who imparted their wisdom to me over the years, thereby allowing me to accumulate the thoughts that I have distilled into this collection of rules. Jim Tynion and Mary Ann Halloin in particular have always been great mentors to me.

I also thank the various proofreaders and unofficial editors, both the volunteers and the "volunteers," with my special thanks to Ann Weilbaecher and Elizabeth Hanigan.

And, of course, I thank my wife for being right all along; I just should have listened to her from the beginning.

FOREWORD

Little that occurs in law school prepares the law gradu-
ate for law practice. While this is a broad indictment of
legal education and, perhaps, law practice, it is a reality that is appreciated only late...or not at all. While it
has become a cliché that law practice is hard, the
degree to which it is both stressful and disorienting
comes as a shock among a disturbingly high percentage
of new lawyers.

In part as a self-criticism of this reality—the treach-
erous transition from student to practitioner—I wrote
The Young Lawyer's Jungle Book, which was intended to
lift the veil over the eyes of the new attorney. It may
well be Lund's book—the one you hold in your hands—
that brings a similar message to a wider, and equally
deserving, audience. (Someone mentioned that I was
crazy to promote, even if indirectly, a "competitor"
book. I had to laugh. First, my allegiance is to the profession and to you; to the extent that either of us can
help, so much the better. Second, I once sent a copy of
my book—at my personal cost, mind you—to another
author, and sure enough, a little more than a year later
another book is released aimed directly at *The Young
Lawyer's Jungle Book.* If anyone deserves the cold shoul-
der, it would not be Lund, who has been unfailingly
polite. As to this other author, by the way, those in
intellectual property will realize the limitations as to
causes of action, and more importantly, those sympa-

JAGGED ROCKS OF WISDOM

thetic to Eastern cultures might wish the other author luck for karmic transgressions.)

Someone else commented, by the way, that I should be upset that Lund has, in essence, "stolen the thunder" of *The Young Lawyer's Jungle Book*. Perhaps. If so, all the more power to him—and to you. My guess, however, is that there's thunder aplenty. My book has a hundred-plus sections. Lund has 21 Rules. Every one of these sections and rules will be helpful to you, in some way at some time...no matter where you practice. And, as Lund states, it's not about him, or me. It's about you. Our perspectives—if I can write for him too—is that our joint contributions were and are to help that large pool of new associates. Quite likely, this includes you.

The Young Lawyer's Jungle Book was criticized for its plainspoken (and at times pointed) tone. I received one letter from a law school dean who wrote that attorneys such as I were what was wrong with the profession. A reviewer wrote that my holding up the realities of law practice for all to view served merely to propagate such unkind practices. Another wrote to complain that I was hardly a reliable source as I had escaped to practice in Honolulu (as indeed I had)...hardly worthy of mention among real cities, I assume.

It is thus refreshing to read advice that is at times even more blunt than mine. Go Lund. Any differences of opinion are minor, and the number of times we paraphrase each other is striking. Some might find Lund's approach both readable and concise, while others might prefer the approach in *The Young Lawyer's Jungle Book*. Perhaps they are thus best read as companions in advice to someone rather important: you. Both Lund and I are direct, however, and neither of us makes apologies. Indeed, it is a source of pride that our "harsh" treatment might—just might—save you *real* harshness, in a partner's office, when the stakes are rather higher.

This is a difficult approach for some to accept, and especially those who have grown comfortable with a saccharine approach to education (and life): no assignment is ever weak, no misstep worthy of critique, no reproach conceivable. The world in which many have grown up over the past two generations is one filled with false praise, false accomplishment, and false excellence. This leads to a false sense of security...a security that will be dashed upon the jagged rocks of the real world of law practice. The impact on your career would be no less devastating, whether or not wisdom is the result.

It is unfortunate that it is up to individuals such as Lund and I—or your future bosses—to set you straight. Yet the real needs of clients are simply too important to accept the unreal world that many new attorneys are used to. And thus, the advice in both books is intended to deliver a difficult message. Shoot the messenger (or Messinger) if you will, but that shan't change the message.

Much of success in any field is in the "soft" side of our skill set. Others in the office—partners, senior associates, senior staff, everyone—will *assume* that you are smart. What they're looking for is that special something else. The satisfaction of a boss—any boss—when they've found someone who knows how to [act, speak, think, drink, chew, console, laugh, you name it].

JAGGED ROCKS OF WISDOM

Lund has hit this social nail on its head: This is exactly the right advice for the new associate. Whether you are ready for it is, of course, up to you. Whether one element of his advice is better at Situation A or Situation B—is also up to you. This is, after all, the essence of law practice: fitting the right theory (and conclusion) to the facts. We cannot tell you *exactly* what to do. Far more important is to raise consciousness about how to proceed, and why. In many office skirmishes, these are the more important preparations.

There is an anecdote (possibly an apocryphal one) about Joe Kennedy, Jr., in which the Kennedy family is reeling from the assassination of the President and then Robert Kennedy. On the train on the way back from the second funeral, Joe was "working the aisle"—not in a pejorative or disrespectful sense, particularly under the grievous circumstances—but in a compassionate way. "I'm Joe Kennedy. Thanks for coming." he would repeat. Ethel Kennedy is said to have remarked, *"He's got it!"* Meaning, he had the extraordinary set of soft skills—political skills—to connect with other individuals, to console them, to be a force. Whether this was appropriate, inappropriate, or simply their way of dealing with grief, Joe's ability transcended the norm, and the train.

In law practice, as in most other arenas, there are three groups of individuals: Those who "have it," those who don't have it, and the large group in the middle who might or might not "get it."

This book—as with *The Young Lawyer's Jungle Book*—was written not for the "natural born" superstars (who are, just perhaps, natural born superstars), or for those who simply cannot or will not accept the social limitations of law practice. Rather, both books are written in triage for the vast middle, for those who *might* do well...but only with help.

How about a story—at my expense—that illustrates this point?

Once upon a time, I had had an especially hard week. Responsible for a staff of some 60 souls, I was, as one might expect, one of the ones who "has it."

I had a flight *very* early in the morning, and had to work quite literally through the night to get a project done. (If that sounds familiar, welcome to law practice.) In getting dressed for the all-day flights, I don't know why but I put on jeans and a nice but not-tucked-in shirt. I was flying with an upgrade, and knew the rules. No problem on the first leg, and no problem on the second flight—except that as I walked away from the counter, the agent called me back and said "Sir, I'm sorry, but I can't let you in First Class with jeans."

Busted.

Now, in my managerial role I will usually decide whether someone is trying to abuse the system or is a first-time offender (as indeed I was here, believe it or not). I decide from there whether to "bust some chops" as an unhappy but needed lesson, yet forgive the transgression—or to deny the outcome.

She was unmoved. Worse, I had thoughtlessly checked in even my carry-on (which had an extra pair of slacks), as the security was recently heightened and I had a hygiene kit that would have been confiscated...so there I was. My assumption was that she should have busted *my* chops a bit, and then said, essentially, "Okay, buster, but never again." She did not, and this, to me, was an excellent lesson as I read this manuscript.

The fault was mine, and the penalty was appropriate. Yes, I wouldn't have responded as she did, and yes, I'd not slept at all and was looking forward to an enjoyable flight, and yes, it's a little silly nowadays as those with real power often wear, well, jeans.

But even so, I broke the rule, and I paid. Simple as that.

I did not "get it." I knew the rule, I decided to disregard the rule, I did not think. My thoughtlessness is analogous to the impact of "rules" in a law office. Break them once and you'll be reminded of the penalties. Break them more than occasionally, and you'll remember the lesson...elsewhere.

That we don't *like* the rules—that we think the rules are silly—that is not the path to take. Yes, the rules sometimes *are* silly. Yes, we can agitate endlessly on the unfairness of it all. Or, we could instead understand those rules—the essence of the law, by the way—and endeavor instead to work within them, rather than in endless battles against them. (And, even if victorious on occasion, there's a reason that battles are fatiguing. Choose *your* battles.)

As is sometimes said, tongue-in-cheek, "If you don't like the law, call your Senator." That should be a guide as to how deeply embedded even these "soft" rules are. Disregard them at your peril.

A postscript to this story: This anecdote connects with me in light of Lund's advice because this happened just about seven hours ago. I am writing this on that very flight, and appreciate with all the more immediacy my error. Upon reflection, it is inappropriate for me to blame the agent for her unyieldingly bureaucratic position. I was looking forward to the flight, which makes my error all the more baffling. The sin was mine—large or small is irrelevant—and I must own the consequences. So too, in a different context, must you.

Another postscript, while we're here: I grew up without money and flew quite frequently in crowded quarters, including numerous flights on People Express, where legroom was left at the gate. This experience was a good way for me to "get off my high horse" and appreciate anew the privileges we—we high-powered attorney types—come to expect.

I hope this anecdote connects with you too, and that you see the lesson as extending to any number of situations. Don't put yourself in situations in which you rely upon the *assumed* kindness of strangers—as with the agent, above. Had I been thinking and walked immediately parallel to the counter, she would never have seen. That's not the point. It's not about "scamming" the system, or about putting our own individualistic needs first. It's about knowing which rules to bend, when, how far, and why. I broke the rule, and I paid. Simple as that.

In this, the social skills to which Lund and I both refer are essential to your success in the law. I accepted this mission—reading and then writing a foreword to *Jagged Rocks of Wisdom*—as an enjoyable way to spend spare hours (my apologies to the publisher for the delays in getting this done in the first place), and indeed it has been enjoyable. To Lund, I extend a voice of thanks, for his contribution to the future generations of junior associates who will be helped in ways large and small, by his efforts and guidance. I agree as well that this advice is not limited to those who intend to work in large firms; this guidance applies to all new professionals, in all offices. It applies especially to law practice, and to law practice in firms.

As always, apply the advice as is appropriate to your circumstance and environment. It is not possible to overstate how important Lund's words are. The specifics of any situation will, of course, depend upon that situation. But your actions and reactions within that situation *are* the issue. Will you respond well, or will you respond poorly? To a large extent, this will depend upon whether you have developed general principles of your actions beforehand, whether you have thought about those principles, and whether you have built up good habits in the meantime.

So, to that group of natural-born superstars, I congratulate you on your good fortune. (I most assuredly do not include myself in this category, by the way.) And

to the group of dedicated individualists and noncon-
formists, I offer not the slightest word of discourage-
ment—but I do encourage you to find an environment
in which you will find happiness. It won't be law practice, at least not in a traditional law office.

And to the vast middle—to that eighty or so percent
of all law graduates—I offer my own experience as
proof of the advice in this book: in life I have failed
where I have not thought, and I have succeeded where
I have. But the "thought" isn't intellectual...it's concep-
tual. When I began law practice I had *no idea* what I
wanted to do—and I wasn't sure that it was law practice.
Fair enough, as that's not uncommon. But the rules
apply nonetheless. The result was my cathartic writing
of *The Young Lawyer's Jungle Book,* and a rather painful
process of discovery, over a years-long period. I wish
such experiences on no one, and thus encourage you to
take the advice in *this* book to heart. In a sense, it's
quite similar to *The Young Lawyer's Jungle Book,* but
written as a three-hour seminar. Few associates are
lucky enough to attend such seminars; here it is, for
you.

To those who are offended by the tone of this book,
I can only shake my head. Not to add offense to injury,
but in thinking about my own reactions to a perceived
need for "niceness."

Nonsense. The lessons in this book are serious, and
the only way that many will get the message is a direct,
here's-the-real-story-kid approach. Years ago I responded to skeptical publishers that, if anything, the tone in
The Young Lawyer's Jungle Book didn't go far enough. In
my mind then, there was no nice way to convey the

message that needed to be conveyed: the sometimes vicious ways of the jungle. So I applaud Lund for his approach. If anything he is even more honest now than I was then. Good for him, and good for you. To reinforce what he says, if you're offended by what he says or how he says it, then take a serious look at your sensitivities: In actual law practice, you will face far, far worse. Better to be offended now (as indeed you should not be), than to face scorn (or worse) before a judge, clerk, senior partner, senior associate, or, yes, secretary.

Be careful out there. There are more traps and more ways to fall into them than can be easily recounted here, or anywhere. And, to borrow from a phrase common in the military, "There is never a time when you're not being observed." Sometimes, it is the ticket agent in life who controls our destiny.

Whatever your flight path in the law, I wish you the very best.

Thane Messinger
Author, *The Young Lawyer's Jungle Book*
November 2006

Introduction:

How to Read This Book

The concept for this book grew out of a presentation I made to a Foley & Lardner LLP summer associate class. The presentation was supposed to be general career advice, but grew into "21 rules" partially out of my wish that somebody had told me these things when I started the practice of law, and partially because I finally had the opportunity to be brutally frank with junior associates in an acceptable setting, thereby venting several years' worth of frustration.

As a result, this book reads more or less like a presentation from a senior attorney to a group of junior attorneys. Rather than attempt to change the approach, the look and the feel, I decided to stay close to the original presentation format. This book should therefore be read from that perspective. The reader should imagine this book as a frank discussion (or even lecture) from a senior attorney. The book is written in the first person, with "I" telling "you" how the world works. The word "partner" is used throughout the book to describe an attorney with authority, which means any attorney more senior than you. In most firms, the "partner" might well be another, more senior associate, but the same rules apply.

The book is written for the "junior attorney." In a larger sense, this encompasses summer associates, law students, junior associates, and also some mid-level associates. Some of the issues described are more applicable to summer associates, others more to practicing attorneys, but all problems and rules apply to at least some extent to each of these groups, and I encourage you to read the whole book with an open mind, without dismissing any discussion as not relevant to your situation.

OFFICIAL DISCLAIMERS

The rules set forth in this book are not unique to any firm, or indeed to the legal profession. While the specifics will vary from firm to firm, the fundamental principles apply in any major law firm, as well as to the higher echelons of many, if not most, larger businesses.

Some of the anecdotes in this book are literal, some are modified to protect the innocent, and some are essentially "combo-anecdotes." Thus, these should be seen not necessarily as literal exchanges but rather as a composite of the collective experiences of my own years as a summer and junior associate as well as those of others with whom I have practiced, along with observations from us all.

Some of the rules set forth herein may strike some readers as obvious and pedantic. If so, I do not apologize, because other readers will find those same rules helpful. Similarly, some rules may strike some readers as unfairly harsh or brutal. If so, I also do not apologize, because that is just too bad. This book is here to be honest, not to be fair. Welcome to the real world. Welcome to law practice.

Further, you will find that many of the rules conflict with each other to some extent, and that it is virtually impossible to comply with one rule without in the process violating another rule.

Again, welcome to reality.

THE RULES

RULE NUMBER 1:

PROOFREAD

There is a reason this is rule number one. Proofreading is essential to the practice of law at every level, and it is particularly crucial to the junior associate. In academic contexts, a distinction is often made between "substantive" and "non-substantive" errors. One speaks of an error being "only a typo." Only "substantive" errors matter.

Forget all of that, and forget it right now.

As a junior associate, it is generally assumed that you have no substantive knowledge or skills. Until you are trained, you are generally useless. As a result, nobody will expect you to produce brilliant legal insights, or take great strategic initiatives. But for the

> *I was wandering about the office one night, seeing who else was working late. I came upon another associate scrambling to assemble proxy materials for a large public company that was about to be acquired. The FedEx deadline was looming, and there was a team of secretaries assembling packages that had to go out that night to all the shareholders of the company (and to several very senior partners of the firm).*
>
> *I sauntered over, picked up a booklet, and started reading from the letter to the shareholders on the cover: "As may you know ..."*
>
> *I was torn between mirth and compassion as all blood drained from my colleague's face.*

same reason, everybody *will* expect you to contribute diligence.

As a result, every single typo brings to mind the following question: "Is he (a) stupid or (b) lazy?" The *only* two reasons we can fathom for why there would be a typo is that either you can't read, or you didn't read. You just didn't try hard enough.

Neither of those alternatives is very flattering.

We know that junior associates will make substantive errors. We dread the errors, but we expect them and we understand them. What really gets us riled up is when somebody does not take the extra time to avoid stupid mistakes.

Proofreading is not simply a matter of impressing the partner, however. Presentation is essential in the practice of law. It is crucial that attorneys instill a sense of confidence in their clients. Imagine yourself the CEO of a Fortune 500 company. You just paid one hundred thousand dollars to your lawyers to have a complex agreement negotiated and drafted, and when you flip to the first page, the name of your company is spelled incorrectly. This does not make you happy.

The importance of proofreading to the junior associate cannot be overstated. If you can be the associate who simply does not have typos, you will be off to an excellent start in your new job. Otherwise, you will have the dreaded "needs to pay attention to detail" attached to your name.

Proofreading is difficult, and will take time to fully master. The first rule for successful proofreading is taking your time. It is much easier to catch errors if you learn to read slowly. Painstakingly. In fact, it may help substantially to let your document sit for a few hours. Do something else, and then come back for the final proofread. If possible, perhaps even leave the document overnight and proofread in the morning (another tip—do not rely on your proofreading skills at 2 a.m.). If you have been reading the document on the computer, print it out. If you have been reading on paper, read it on the screen. Use search functions to find terms. Have your friends double-check your work. Be imaginative. But do not forget to proofread.

Rule Number 2:

Proofread Again

I should make it absolutely clear—proofreading is *very* important. Take proofreading exceedingly seriously.

Proofreading is not merely a matter of avoiding misspelled words, however. Check your sentence structure. If writing a memo or a brief, make sure your cites are correct. If writing an agreement, make sure your defined terms and cross-references are correct.

And *always* spell the client's name correctly.

Some of the reasons for proofreading are not always apparent. Some things just do not seem important enough, and perhaps just are not important enough. But remember that everything you write will be read. Many times. By many people. Many many people. Many many judgmental people. For a long time. For a very long time.

When I was a fourth-year associate, a fellow associate in a different department told me she had some questions for me. When I got to her office she pulled out an old memo to show to me. Imagine my horror when I realized that I had written the memo when I was a summer associate. My friend was asking for clarification of something I had written. Five years ago. As a fresh summer associate. And, of course, the memo was riddled with typos, poor grammar and questionable logic. Did my friend notice? I don't see how not.

When in school, your paper is a private matter between you and your professor. Were you ever embarrassed to show your paper to other students? You had better get over that. The practice of law is a community effort, and is always in the public eye. Nothing you do is for the benefit of the partner alone. After she is done with your memo, she passes it on to other members of the case team, she passes it on to the client, and she keeps a copy in her file. And then, three years later when she is on another, similar case, she pulls out the old memo and recirculates it again.

Nothing ever goes away, and nothing is ever private. If you are on a large transaction, every little email you send out will be read by 20 people or more, and those emails all stay in the file, and will be reviewed if (or when) that transaction is litigated ten years later.

> *During most of my associate career, I worked maintenance on a finance deal that closed when I was a freshman in college. Over the course of the work with the file, I became intimately familiar with the work of each of the attorneys on the original transaction. At one point I had nicknames for several of the major players. When I finally met some of these people, now senior attorneys at other firms, it was all I could do not to giggle when remembering some of the strange things they had written in their memos ten years earlier.*

In today's law office, a junior associate has access to a wonderful tool to aid in the proofreading: The spell-check function on your word processor. Simply hit "F7" (or whichever) and voila! Your document is error-free.

Were it only so easy.

There are two things to remember about the spell-checker: Use it, and distrust it.

First, the spell-checker is a wonderful tool. It can spot mistakes that your sleep-deprived eyes cannot. It can help compensate for your lack of attention in the third grade. To fail to use this tool is a grave mistake, for two reasons: failing to use the spell-checker will result in more errors, which is bad enough, and failing to use the spell-checker will result in errors that obviously (to the reviewing partner) would have been caught by a spell-checker. The presence of this error, therefore, will convince the partner that not only did you not proofread properly, but you are too lazy even to hit "F7".

The second thing to remember is that the spell-checker is no substitute for your proofreading skills. It is there to help you, not to do your job for you. "Sorry, the spell-checker didn't catch that" is no excuse for an error in a document. Run spell-check several times during your proofreading, and then proofread what the computer changed, to make sure that it is still correct. It is YOUR job to proofread—the spellchecker is just there to help you.

A corollary of this is to avoid the use of the "change all" function when spell-checking. This is just asking for trouble. You need to personally approve each and every change in your document. What is a typo in one instance may be perfectly legitimate in another, and you need to make that decision yourself.

The same principle applies to all types of "replace all" functions. The client changed its name, and you need to change that name dozens of times in a large filing? Do not use "replace all". You may discover the hard way that your client's name appears inside other words, or that an affiliate of your client has a name very similar to your client, or that there was an historical reference that needed to stay with the old spelling. Just don't do it. You are the decider of what goes into your document. Do not abdicate that responsibility to a machine.

This also applies in other automated document revisions. Most large documents have a table of contents that is automatically generated and updated by the computer. Guess what—you are responsible for errors in the table of contents as well, even though you didn't write it. So print it out and check it. Use the print preview functions. Do whatever you have to do, but make sure that the computer didn't slip one by you. Do you like to use automatic section cross-references? That's great—so long as you check all the cross-references after the computer is done updating them. The computer usually gets the cross-references right. In law school, "usually" gets you an A. In law practice, "usually" gets you sued for malpractice.

Rule Number 3:

Everything Is Your Fault

This rule is my personal favorite. Imagine: You are working on a memo, and you hand your secretary a heavy markup. She makes the changes and hands the document to the partner, who is not pleased with the number of typos in the document. Whose fault is it?

Yours.

You are sending documents to the copy shop for reproduction and binding. The documents come back out of order, and the client is upset because the documents are not the way they are supposed to be. Whose fault is it?

Yours.

You are working on a brief, and the filing deadline is tomorrow. Suddenly your computer crashes, and your document is lost. The filing deadline is missed, and the suit dismissed. Whose fault is it?

Yours.

An earthquake collapses your office building, burying your entire office. Your document is lost. Whose fault is it?

Okay, maybe not this one. But just about everything short of an earthquake is *your* fault. No *ifs*, no *ands*, no *buts*. Your fault. Every time. Law firms function on strict liability. If you touched a project, and anything goes wrong with that project, it is your fault. Causality is irrelevant.

Actually, perhaps "fault" is the wrong word. Maybe "responsibility" is better. The reason for this rule is quite simple. If your task is to get me "A", then your task is to get me "A". Not to *try* for "A", not to *see* if you can accomplish "A", but simply to *get* "A". At that point the universe is divided in two: "A", and "not-A". Anything that isn't "A" is "not-A", and will not make me happy. I don't care why you gave me "not-A", all I know is that I now have "not-A" when I specifically asked for "A". Reasons, causes, excuses, good intentions—all are irrelevant and uninteresting to me. Get me "A".

The reason for this, of course, is that you're not special. This reasoning applies to everybody—not just you. When the suit gets dismissed because your computer broke, the partner has to call the client and tell him that

As a junior associate I was charged with arranging the copying and collating of documents for daily distribution to the transaction working group for the complex transaction I was working on. This task mostly involved me carrying documents to and from the copying center. It was essentially impossible for me to double-check the volume of copying/collating being done. Thousands of pages would go out each day.

One day the partner called me into her office, where she explained to me—in greater detail than I care to remember—just how important attention to detail was: Two pages were missing from one document in the previous night's distribution. No small matter, this. Those two pages might have been crucial to the client's interest—and their omission might have landed both the partner and me into seriously scalding water.

the suit was dismissed. Will the client care why the suit was dismissed? Of course not. The client is unhappy, and will be even more unhappy when the bill shows up. All the client knows is that his suit was dismissed, when he asked your firm to take care of things. Most definitely "not-A."

To put things in a more personally relevant context, imagine your wedding day. Presumably a rather important day for you. Everything is great. Except that there is no wedding cake. You specifically ordered a cake, but there is no cake. Do you care *why* there is no cake? Are you interested in hearing about the baker's car trouble, health problems, broken computer, or anything else at all? Or do you simply want wedding cake? At that point your world is divided in two possibilities: Cake and No Cake. The *why* is irrelevant.

So what do you do? How do you cope with a job where everything is your fault, even things apparently beyond your control? You remember Rule #1, and Proofread. Everything. Then you remember Rule #2, and you Proofread Everything Again. Double-check everything you do. Do not assume that the copy shop did it correctly; do not assume that your secretary knew the right address for the package. Nothing is correct until you have personally seen that it is correct.

Also remember that there is only one definition of "correct"—and that is whatever the partner says it is. If you hand me a document that I do not like, it is *not* a valid excuse that "Partner *x*" likes her documents this way. I am not Partner *x*, and I do not care how she likes her documents. I want my documents the way *I* like them, and it is your job to make that happen. Period.

Rule Number 4:

Be Socially Aware

This rule, while absolutely crucial, is also amorphous, confusing, vague, and tricky. When you enter the offices of a large law firm, it is easy to be swayed by the corporate trappings—offices, secretaries, receptionists, all manner of hustle and bustle. But despite the apparent corporate machinery, a law firm is nothing but a collection of people, a collection of individuals. These individuals are vastly different from each other, and each must be treated accordingly.

A law firm is also a more varied environment than you may be accustomed to. In academia, there are students, most of whom are about the same age, and there are professors, most of whom are about the same age. On the side, there are administrators. Three distinct classes, each fairly homogenous within itself. In a law firm, there will be people born the same year as you, people born the same year as your grandparents, and every year in between. The "classes" of people are at once very distinct and very muddled. There might be people only a year or two older than you (or perhaps even younger than you) who will be your direct supervisor, and there will be people thirty years older than you who now work for you.

And unlike school, it is important for you to function well with *all* of them. You cannot be rude to the "uncool kids," you cannot marginalize the "professors." *Everyone* is important. It is essential that you become socially

A first-year associate who was very self-confident was summoned to a partner's office. The associate casually plopped himself in a chair and put his feet on her desk.
She preferred her desk without feet, and the associate never got any work from her again.

aware—pay attention to the behavior of those around you. Understand the interpersonal dynamics and interaction styles. Lawyers can be touchy at times, and you do not want to offend anybody.

That is tricky.

In fact, it is so tricky that you should stick to a few simple guidelines: do not play office politics. Nothing good can come of it, and you do not have the information (or, to be blunt, power) to do it well. Treat people the way *they* want to be treated, not the way *you* want to be treated. The golden rule—doing unto others as you would wish they do unto you—works in all directions in law firms. When in doubt, err on the side of more courtesy and more formality—it is easy to back off the formality, but almost impossible to regain lost ground. Individuality is great, but this is not the time to show everybody just how special you are. In general, just behave like your mother taught you and things will be fine.

There is a reason this rule is called "Be Socially *Aware*" and not "Employ Social Skills." We know you have social skills. The problem many junior associates face is that they employ the wrong set of social skills. They forget their surroundings, or fail to observe their surroundings in the first place. Remember where you are, and whom you are around. Observe the behavior of those around you and adjust your own behavior accordingly.

> *A summer associate was enjoying his new paycheck, and had ordered some collectable memorabilia to be delivered to his office. Interestingly, he didn't collect teapots or doilies, but WWII replica machine guns. Few other offices had such period weaponry.*

In school, indeed in most of your life up to this point, you could surround yourself with like-minded people. In essence, you could adjust your surroundings to suit yourself. That approach will no longer work, if you intend to work in the law. While nobody expects you to be a conformist drone, and individuality (to a point) is encouraged, there is a limit. This is not the time to loudly proclaim how unique you are. Do not get an outlandish haircut. Do not sing loudly in the bathroom. Watch the behavior of other attorneys. Do they keep their office doors open most of the time? Yes? Then you should keep yours open as well. Do they work with headphones on? No? Then neither should you. Be *aware* of your surroundings.

Similarly, there is no need to pick a fight. Lawyers as a group enjoy a spirited discussion, but the rules differ from law school discussions. You do not wade into a group of hard-core Republicans and loudly proclaim that Republicans are all idiots. That may be a suitable discussion technique in law school (or at least in junior high school), but not in a law firm. Your intelligent

> *Over the years I have seen summer associates not get offers because they wouldn't wear suits when required, because they looked at their feet and mumbled, because they drank too much, because they complained too much, because they verbally assaulted other summer associates, and for just being too darn arrogant.*

commentary might be appreciated; your abrasively aggressive behavior will not.

Also consider working hours. Law firms are strictly "flex time." Usually this means you work all the time, but you do have *some* control and discretion with regard to your schedule. This does not, however, mean that you can elect to work second shift. Be socially aware. Do most people in the office seem to work 8:30 to 6:00, more or less? Then maybe it is not a good idea to come in at 9:30 every day. Do not model yourself after the senior partner who comes in just in time to go to lunch. He has earned that right; you have not.

One more sub-item deserves an honorable mention: the dress code. What constitutes appropriate dress in the office is constantly in flux, and there is a fairly wide range in today's offices. It can be particularly tricky for women to hit just the right level of dress. The solution? Be socially aware. There are some things for which you want to be noticed, and other things for which you want to blend in. Being known as the sloppy dresser is not a good way to start. See what the people around you are wearing. Then match the dress of the average-to-formal people. Do not emulate the casual dresser.

Remember, you are being judged every day. Many people—even those with whom you might never work—will judge you entirely based on whether your pants are pressed. Do not give anyone an excuse to dislike you.

Rule Number 5:

Just Say No to Preliminary Reports

This problem comes in two varieties: the elevator report, and the draft memo.

The Elevator Report: you get in the elevator one morning, and just as the doors close, in walks the partner for whom you are just writing a research memo. The memo is due tomorrow. As the elevator heads up to the office, the partner strikes up some small talk. At about the 20th floor, she asks you how the memo is coming. "Fine," you say. (Of course.) And then, as you can practically hear the theme chords from *Jaws* in the background, she asks what you think the conclusion will be.

Do not answer.

That does not mean you should stand there like an idiot—but don't *be* an idiot and give her your guess as to what the research will reveal. If your research isn't done, you might discover the hard way that there was a reason your research was not done. If you think your research is done, you are wrong—your research isn't done until the memo is done. Many research errors and oversights are discovered only when attempting to put a conclusion in writing. There are only two states of research: "done" and "not done."

This is when you have to apply Rule Number 4: Be Socially Aware. Dance the line: "I don't really have a firm conclusion yet," or "I have not completed the research yet, and I am not comfortable telling you something that might be wrong," or perhaps even, if you really have to, "there are some cases that support our position, but there also appears to be some authority against our position." Do *not* under any circumstances utter the following phrase, or anything like it: "I think my conclusion will be *x*."

> *When I was a first-year associate a very senior partner asked me to research a matter of partnership liability. One day in the elevator, when my research was 90% complete and the memo almost done, he asked me what I had found. I told him what the expected result of the research was.*
>
> *As I finished up the research and the memo, I found the one final case that I had missed before. The correct answer was the exact opposite of what I had told the partner. I quickly rushed my memo to completion (now replete with typos) to get it to the partner, but by now he had already told the client the "good news." He was NOT thrilled that he had to call the client back to reverse the verdict. He was even less thrilled with my typo-filled "draft" memo.*
>
> *It was years before I worked for that partner again.*

Version two of preliminary reports is the Draft Memo, also known as "just give me what you've got": you dodged the partner in the elevator, and it is now the following day. The partner is itching for the memo, and tells you to just give her what you have—don't worry, she knows that it is a draft, and it isn't complete, and don't worry about the typos.

She is lying. Do not do it.

Here again, apply Rule #4. Delicately explain that the memo will be done shortly, but do not give her an incomplete document. There are only two states of documents: "done" and "not done."

The reasoning behind Rule #5 is simple. You will be judged on your work product, regardless of how it is labeled. If the elevator report turns out to be incorrect, you are now a sloppy researcher. If the draft memo has typos, you are a poor writer. In a law firm, nothing is ever erased. That draft memo with the typos will be in the partner's files until judgment day, and every time someone looks at it, they will think you are an idiot. Worse yet, most large firms have a formal evaluation procedure. Your sloppy "draft" memo will be mentioned in your written evaluation, which goes in your file, where it is revisited every time you are evaluated—forever.

There is a corollary to Rule #5: Make everything you touch as perfect as humanly possible before you pass it on. Everything. Every time. You will be judged on everything that leaves your desk, and everything that leaves your mouth. There is never a time you are not being observed. Make sure that your work product is absolutely perfect. Every time. The reason is simple: Rule #3—Everything is Your Fault.

This, of course, leads us right back to Rule #1—Proofread. And after that, Rule #2—Proofread Again.

Unfortunately, following Rule #5 is difficult. Painfully, mind-numbingly, sometimes excruciatingly difficult. Some senior attorneys have forgotten this rule, and fully expect preliminary reports, and fully expect them to be correct. In this case, you need to employ Rule #4—Be Socially Aware. Understand the attorney you are working for, and understand their expectations. Some partners will accept an outright "I don't feel comfortable giving a preliminary conclusion at this time," but others will be horribly offended by such cheekiness. Every senior attorney is different, and they all expect different things from you. It is up to you to determine what each and every one of them wants.

Rule Number 6:

Take It Seriously—Because It *Is*

This is no longer the classroom. The assignments you are given are not make-work. Real decisions involving real money will be made based on your work. Even general research for "internal use," which is not relevant to any immediate case, will eventually be used by somebody, sometime, in some serious way. Once again, therefore, make absolutely *certain* that everything that leaves your desk is as perfect as it can possibly be. Remember Rule #1—Proofread, and Rule #2—Proofread Again.

Similarly, any document you draft may well be sent on to the client, whether you intended it to or not. You should therefore treat every little piece of work you do as essential—because it is. If your job is to copy some documents, copy well. If the correct copies do not get where they need to be, significant financial loss could be the result. There are no unimportant tasks. And remember Rule #3—Everything is Your Fault.

Act accordingly.

The nonchalant attitude that some summer associates have, and even some permanent associates, never ceases to amaze me. They treat the job like a game, or a puzzle to be solved. Granted, we are not physicians, and it is unlikely that people will die if we mess up, but that does not make the job a game.

And if you cannot take your clients' business seriously, take your own job seriously. Few things will upset a partner faster than an associate who does not take *his* client seriously. If you are to work on *my* deal, you need to convince *me* that you are taking the deal seriously, because I can promise you that I take it very

> *When I was a summer associate, a senior partner in the corporate department gave me what appeared to be a fairly simple research project. He explained that a competitor of one of our larger clients had been found liable in a class action suit for $500,000,000. Apparently one of the form agreements used by this competitor did not meet certain consumer disclosure requirements in certain states. The equivalent form agreement that our client used also did not meet these requirements, but it was not clear whether the require- ments actually applied to our agreements. I was to determine whether our client should change their form agreement, or proceed with the existing form.*
>
> *After a couple of hours of research, I concluded that these consumer requirements did not apply, and no change was needed. I went to the partner's office and told him what I had found. Upon hearing my report, he turned around and—with me in the office—called the general counsel at this very large company. As my blood pressure rose, the partner told the general coun- sel that she did not need to take any action, as our research had determined that their contracts were not subject to the requirement in question.*
>
> *And thus, based on two hours of my research, a decision was made that was potentially worth half a billion dollars.*
>
> *This got my attention.*

seriously indeed. A lackadaisical attitude will shine through loud and clear, and will significantly shorten your career prospects.

Rule Number 7:
This Is Not School; This Is Not Homework

Many summer associates find themselves approaching the summer internship with an exam mentality. This approach is quickly validated (inadvertently) by the attorneys and recruiting coordinators at the firm. You are quickly told about obtaining "assignments" and completing "projects" by the "due date." The terminology is almost academic in nature. This could easily encourage you to approach your summer internship— or your associate position—like you approached school.

Don't.

This job is most definitely not school, and the assignments are most definitely not homework. The principles are entirely different. With homework in school, you can take the B. You can decide what is "good enough," and take your chances with the grades. After all, as long as you are in the top quartile of your class, you will probably get a decent job. When writing a paper for school, you get to decide the content, the style, and the conclusion, and you get to decide when it is complete.

None of this applies to your new job as an attorney.

Your assignment is done when *I* say it is done. You do not get a say. If I do not like your style, you change your style. All assignments on the job are pass/fail. There are no intermediate grades, and the passing grade is one hundred percent.

If you do not get 100%, you do it over—and over—and over—until you *do* get 100%. Anything less is unacceptable.

And only I get to decide when we are at 100%.

The reason, again, is simple. Our clients pay us for product "A." They don't pay for product "90%-of-A," or product "99%-of-A." It is either "A" or "not-A," and "99%-of-A" might as well be "0%-of-A." 99% is better than 50% only because it will take less work to get up to 100%. Ultimately, everything gets to 100%. Nothing goes to the client until it is 100%.

A corollary of this rule is that since the definition of "100%" exists only in the partner's head, it is almost guaranteed that, no matter how excellent your work product, the assigning attorney will have comments. *Many* comments. Most go years before they see a document without comments. Act accordingly.

A classic summer associate move that you should *not* repeat is to hand in your last assignments of the summer on your last day at the firm. Invariably, of course, the partner will have comments. She forgot that Friday was your last day, and comes looking for you on Monday with comments. You, of course, are long gone, and have accomplished two things: (a) your final work product of the summer is imperfect, and (b) the partner spent much of the day Saturday revising your work, which did not endear you to her. As a result, that Friday may very well have been your very last day at the firm—literally.

As a summer associate, finish your projects a day or two in advance of your last day, and remind everybody you are working for that you are leaving. As a permanent associate, understand the transaction/case schedule, and know that there needs to be time for revisions. Always follow up. Do not pester the partner, but sometimes things slip down the to-do list. If you do not hear back in a day or two, make a quick visit to ask if you can be of further assistance, or if he had any comments on your memo.

Remember, your job is not done until the *partner* decides that your assignment is 100% done.

Rule Number 8:

Form *And* Substance—Display Confidence

So you wrote the perfect memo, you proofread it seven times, double-checked your research, dropped it off at the partner's office, wiped the sweat off your forehead, and sat down in your office for a break. An hour later (or a day, or a week), the partner calls you into his office. The conversation begins "Well, I read your memo...." and then it's off to the races. The partner proceeds to grill you on how you reached conclusion X in the memo, and whether you consulted source Y. (You did consult source Y, yes?) He further asks how your conclusion will be affected by fact Z (which of course you didn't know about). The inquisition continues. Yet at the end, the partner does not appear horribly dissatisfied with your memo.

This is a common example of how presentation is as important as content. For you to be successful in a project—any project—you have to accomplish two things. First, you have to generate the correct answer, the per-

There were some partners who frightened me for years. Even as a mid-level associate, I found myself breaking into a sweat when they called. It took everything I had to look them in the eye, to not mumble and stutter, and to speak loudly, clearly, and concisely. It was only when I realized that I really did know what I was talking about that I was able to keep my voice under control.

fect document, whatever. Second, and equally important, you have to convince the partner that you have generated the correct answer, or the perfect document.

Remember that Rule #3—Everything is Your Fault—applies to partners as well as to junior associates. The partner has to risk her reputation and career on the content of *your* document, and she is just trying to decide if you are worth that risk. If you are unable to convince the partner that your result is reliable, she will now have to either redo the work herself, or get another associate (whom she *does* trust) to do it (again) for her. Neither outcome will reflect well on you.

Much of this trust is built up over time, but much is also conveyed in the presentation of a document or a result. A well-written memorandum will be its own best argument. It will convey confidence in the result, and justify that result thoroughly and carefully. A memorandum that simply provides the answer is useless. Unless you can convince the reader that you know what you are talking about, the result is meaningless. Remember, this is for real. The partner doesn't have the teacher's edition to check the answer—he is relying on you.

For this reason, when the partner is grilling you—in fact, treat *every* partner interaction this way—speak as if you are writing a memo. Make every sentence clear, every thought complete. Structure your argument, and speak deliberately. It is essential that you (a) have confidence in your product, and (b) convey that confidence. If you tend to stutter, don't. If you speak too fast, slow down. If you mumble, speak up. You should maintain eye contact and strong body language. Do not slouch and do not fidget. You are now a big-time lawyer—act the part. If you have confidence in your work product, do not be afraid to show that confidence. If you do not have confidence in your work product, go back and work on it some more.

*But...*there is a fine but crucial line between confident and arrogant. Confidence is good—arrogance is a career-killer. Be honest with the partner, but also with yourself.

There is a practice tip worth mentioning here. When writing or speaking, be specific, and avoid pronouns when possible. "He sent it to them after he got the letter from Bill" is not a good sentence. Remember that the partner was probably thinking of a completely different transaction until you walked in her door, and probably has absolutely no idea what you are talking about. A better sentence would be "John Smith, the Vice President at Cisco, told me that he FedEx'ed the draft Information Memorandum to CitiBank after he received the reminder letter from Bill at Morgan Stanley." In English class, you can use all the pronouns you want. In the law office, do not.

RULE NUMBER 9:

ADMIT ERRORS—SADLY

Okay...you screwed up. It was bound to happen, with six people telling you to do eleven things, all at the same time. Or perhaps you did not screw up, but your secretary screwed up, or FedEx screwed up. Same thing.

Now what?

First, tell the truth. Ignoring a mistake is a sure way to get yourself in a lot of trouble, quickly. Actively *hiding* the ball is a sure way to get yourself fired, quickly. When you see a problem or a mistake, address the problem—do not ignore it. One axiom of the practice of law is that all errors are uncovered, without fail. Eventually it all comes out. Another axiom of the practice of law is that mistakes grow like cancer when ignored.

But this is where an important application of Rule #4—Be Socially Aware—comes in. Errors are bad. Partners do not like errors, because they have to explain errors to the clients, and clients *really* do not like errors. But you still have to tell the partner. Be a man—or a woman, as the case may be—and fess up. March right into the partner's office and tell him you made a mistake. Do not leave a voicemail, do not send an email, do not send your secretary to give the bad news. Do it yourself.

Just remember that errors are bad. The partner is going to be unhappy when you tell him of the mistake. He will be *very* unhappy if you are nonchalant about it.

A summer associate I worked with one year continuously failed to complete and turn in a memorandum. Over the course of several weeks he successively blamed his computer, the firm's server, his secretary, and—no kidding—his dog (which ate the only existing copy).

He did not receive an offer.

You need to convey to the partner your sincere (and it must be sincere!) regret and concern. Remember Rule #6—Take it Seriously, Because it *Is*—and do not act like this is no big deal. Anything less than perfection *is* a *big* deal. You *should* feel bad—you screwed up. Do not go in and start sobbing, but do make sure the partner knows that you are upset about this as well. A little nervous sweat is a good thing.

Most experienced attorneys are used to dealing with mistakes—we are, after all, decent problem-solvers. Following a brief moment of glaring, and maybe the occasional swearing, the immediate concern among nearly all partners will be to fix the problem. Few partners will be out to "punish" you. But once the fix is completed, the partner may begin to consider your mistake, and the likelihood of it happening again. If you conveyed nonchalance to the partner about your mistake, he will take from that that you do not truly care, and that you therefore will not give 100% effort, and that you therefore cannot be trusted, and that you therefore should not be given any more work.

All because you did not look nervous enough.

Now, beyond simply looking terrified, there are some other things you can do to help your situation. First, do not point fingers. Do not blame the secretary, the weather, FedEx, or your dog. Ever. Because, of course, Rule #3—Everything is Your Fault. Fingerpointing will only anger the partner further and make you look worse.

In addition, go in with a plan. "I'm sorry, Bill, but we missed the filing deadline" is okay, but this is better: "I'm sorry, Bill, but we missed the filing deadline. I did, however, check the agency regulations, and we can file up to five days late for an additional fee." That is *much* better. It is better for the client (and therefore the partner) because the problem is getting fixed. It is also better for you, because you showed that (a) you cared, (b) you recognized the problem, and (c) you took the initiative to find out the fix, thereby (d) minimizing the stress on the partner.

But when trying to find a way to fix your problem, consider Rule #13—Don't Exceed Your Authority. Do not *make* the late filing—the *partner* needs to know and decide. Do not call the SEC begging for an extension—you might aggravate the problem instead of fixing it. Make sure the partner knows what is going on.

Rule Number 10:

Take a Load Off—Your Supervisor

One of the best ways to become a successful attorney is to create for yourself a reliable source of work. That way you will be busy, and will keep your job. The best way to do this is repeat business. The best way to get repeat business is to do a good job.

Sounds simple and obvious? One would think so, but this principle is ignored, violated, and utterly disregarded...constantly. Amazing.

As a junior associate, most of your day consists of attacking tasks that you do not fully understand—tasks which were given to you by somebody who presumably does understand them. As a direct result, there is a tendency to fall into the safety-net trap. "Well, I'm not sure about this provision, but I am sure that [the partner] will catch it and fix it."

Big mistake.

The partner did not give you work as an exercise. She gave you work because she wanted you to do it. More specifically, the partner did not want to do it herself. Therefore, when the partner reviews your document, she does not want to have to do more than is absolutely necessary to it. If the partner spends almost as much time correcting your work as she would have simply doing it herself, there is a good chance that that is exactly what will happen the next time.

So what do you do?

Well, first remember Rules #1 and #2—Proofread, and then Proofread again. But more specifically, take the document as far as you can. The partner is your client—she is paying you to fix a problem, or to create a document. Turning that responsibility back to the partner is not a job well done.

As a first-year associate, I had been asked to revise some documents, which would be shipped to the client that evening. After much hard work, I proudly showed up at the partner's door 15 minutes before shipping cutoff with the completed documents. I proceeded to ask the partner "where are the shipping labels?" He was not happy that I had not proactively considered the shipping logistics. By not arranging for labels on my own, I had failed to reduce his burden.

Specifics:

• Fill in the blanks. Complete the names, the dates, whatever. Why leave the blanks for the partner to look up the proper name of the company, or the date of the contract? That is your job.

• Ask questions. If you do not know something (which will happen), do not ignore your ignorance and assume the partner will fix it. Insert a comment or question in the document, or knock on the partner's door and obtain additional guidance or information. Or, better yet, impose on a senior associate to help you, without even bothering the partner.

• Think ahead. What is the next step? Can you get started on the next task without being told (just don't exceed your authority), thereby helping the whole deal along?

You were given work to *reduce* the amount of work for your supervisor, not simply pass it back, and certainly not create additional work for the partner. When you are about to hand something back, ask yourself—truly—whether you moved the ball forward or simply made a lateral pass. The partner is your client. Ask yourself whether you earned your paycheck on *that* project.

Rule Number 11:

The Partner Is Always Right—Usually

A law firm is not a democracy.

It is a common belief among summer associates and junior associates that they have an equal say in decisions regarding their projects.

Wrong.

There are two ways of doing things: The partner's way, and the wrong way. You are allowed and encouraged to voice your opinion, but only once. Few things will enrage a senior attorney faster than having to negotiate with a junior attorney. If your opinion is overruled, it is overruled. There are no appeals.

As a junior associate, I once found myself working with a very senior partner. It was a small transaction, and I had significant authority. As a result, I placed a lot of personal stake in the content of the documents. On one occasion, however, the partner had an issue with my choice of words in a particular section. I defended my choice of words, not wanting to cede control of the document.

In retrospect, I can practically see the smoke coming out of the partner's ears as his "suggestions" for language improvement became firmer and firmer. I, on the other hand, thought we were having a fine discussion. Finally, after some back and forth (more than I would tolerate now myself), the partner explicitly (and loudly) ordered me to do it his way.

And there is good reason for this.

Do not forget that of the two people in the room, only one has years and years of experience, and that person is not you. Do not forget that there is almost certainly a reason why the partner wants it just so, and just because you do not understand it or because she does not tell you what it is does not make it any less valid or accurate. Give the partner the benefit of the doubt. You will be surprised, again and again, at how much those old geezers really do know. You may not realize it until much later, but the overwhelming majority of the time, the partners *are* right.

And if you do not or will not accept the wisdom and experience of the partner, simply accept her authority. She is the boss, and you are not. So just do it.

If you honestly think the partner made a mistake (which, believe it or not, may happen), and you are really *really* confident, point it out to her. But if she tells you that you are wrong, then you are wrong, and you should do it her way. And remember, do not think of a partner's "suggestions" as mere suggestions. Partners do not suggest—even if couched in gentle terms—they order.

Rule Number 12:

Ask Stupid Questions, Not Lazy Questions

A common lie you will hear from partners is some version of the following: "Ask me anything—there are no stupid questions." This statement is usually well-intended, but unfortunately almost always false.

It is important to remember Rule #4—Be Socially Aware. Even if the questions you are asking are not all that stupid, at some point stupid questions become annoying questions. While the partner wants to help and guide you, there is a limit to her patience. She has work to do as well, and it does not include giving you a head start on next year's Civil Procedure class. Ask the questions you need to ask, but watch for cues that you may be wearing out your welcome.

More important still is to avoid the lazy question.

We know you do not know much about anything yet, but we expect you to try—Remember Rule #10—Take a Load Off. It is one thing to ask us for help—it is another thing entirely to ask us to do the work we just assigned to you.

Educate yourself before asking a question. Look for the answer. Read the contract, visit the library. If you ask me a question, and I can casually flip to Section 2.1 of the contract that I asked you to review and find the answer, I will not be happy.

For example:

BAD: "What section of Article IX applies to this problem?"

GOOD: "I think section 9-316 applies here. Does that make sense?"

One of those is a stupid question; the other is just plain lazy. We can cure you of stupid; lazy is forever. A fine quote to summarize this point is to remember to "open book before mouth."

A caveat is in order. *Always* remember Rule #4—Be Socially Aware. Every partner is different. Some partners have a repressed desire to be law professors, and would love to lecture on the finer points of Article IX all day. Others have a veneer-thin tolerance for questions of any kind, and expect you to figure out everything on your own. You need to learn—from personal cues and office gossip—who likes to be treated how.

Rule Number 13:

Keep Supervisors Informed—Don't Exceed Your Authority

This rule has two parts: (1) do not be a loose cannon, and (2) do not be an unguided missile.

Take these two parts in reverse order. First, seek guidance: If your project is lengthy, check in from time

> *My very first assignment as a summer associate was a bankruptcy research project for a senior partner. I got the assignment on Tuesday, and the memo was due on Friday. This was a tight timeline, particularly since I knew nothing about bankruptcy. I consulted with a fellow summer associate who had taken a bankruptcy course (thereby cleverly deploying Rule #15), but still had a hard time with the project. Determined to be the engine that could, I worked until 3 am Friday morning to finish the memo on time. Proud and exhausted I went home for a 3-hour nap before returning to the office, only to discover that the partner was out of the office, and would not be back for several days. It would have made absolutely no difference if I had worked on the memo over the weekend.*
>
> *I did not know that because I had not spoken to the partner since she assigned me the project. Had I even stopped by her office once, she would have told me that she would be out. Should she have tracked me down to tell me that Friday was no longer a strict deadline? She could have, but I was working for her, not the other way around. It was my responsibility to keep track of my project, and I paid the price for failure.*

to time to make sure you are on track. You do not want to finish a great project, only to find that you did something different (or differently) than what the partner wanted. Things can—and will—change, and you do not want to be left out of the loop on what is going on.

While adhering to this rule, however, do not fall into the trap of violating Rule #5. Checking in should not be confused with a preliminary report. You can give a status report, and a progress report, but not a preliminary conclusion.

Checking in on larger assignments will also give the partner significant peace of mind. Few things will give the partners the jitters like wondering how you are doing on the contract, or *if* you are working on the contract. Simply letting him know that you are making progress will score you points.

Second, understand the limits on your authority. Here is a bright-line rule that applies in most, if not all, law firms: As a summer associate, do not contact anyone—anyone at all—outside the firm, in any fashion at all, without explicit authorization and instructions from a senior attorney. As a junior associate, this rule is only slightly less strict—you will have to learn the limits and live by them.

This prohibition includes calling the client, opposing counsel, regulators, newspapers, shareholders, or anyone else you might come into contact with. Do not call them, do not converse with them, do not send them emails. You do not have the experience, or the information, to know that you are doing the right thing—and doing the wrong thing can be a disaster.

Don't do it.

A summer associate was working on a large transaction for a publicly traded company. She had a good understanding of the transaction, and was doing fairly high-level research about filing requirements. At one point she was stumped. The SEC rulings were vague, and she figured she would go to the source for clarification. So she called the SEC. Understanding the risks involved, she called anonymously, and did not identify the client or transaction. However, in order to get a meaningful answer from the regulator, she provided a fairly detailed (if generic) description of the transaction. Needless to say, there were only so many transactions of this nature active at the time, and the regulator immediately knew exactly which transaction was at hand. The beans were spilled, the SEC knew more than was intended, and significant problems were created.

Remember, everything you do reflects upon the firm. As far as the outside world is concerned you *are* the firm. Act accordingly.

Finally, of course, when applying this rule, always remember Rule #4—Be Socially Aware. Know your partner. One partner you work for may expect a voice-mail each and every day with a report on the day's activities—even if absolutely nothing happened. Anything less and his stress level will rise by the minute. On the other hand, other partners will take the "tell me when you are done" approach, and get annoyed by excessive follow up. Most are somewhere in between.

Rule Number 14:

The Partner Is Not Your Friend

As a summer associate, the schmooze is on. You are invited to partners' homes, you go to lunch with senior attorneys, play golf with the department chair, and hang out at the bar with the CEO. Even after you start your full-time job, you see the partners at the bar at every retreat and every closing dinner, and still play golf with the partners at outings. You shoot the breeze, discuss politics, the weather, their kids' college choices, and all around have a grand old time.

Come to think of it, partners are just fun people to hang out with.

Do not let them fool you.

Yes, partners are fun to hang out with. Yes, they are interesting, and witty, and all that good stuff. Yes, they are being nice to you, and ask about your fiancée and your law school experience.

But, no, they are not your friends.

Come Monday morning, it is back to the office, and you are theirs to order around. Just because he gave you a pointer on your putting on Saturday afternoon does *not* mean that he wants to chitchat on Monday morning. Furthermore, it definitely does not mean that he wants you to interrupt his conversation with another partner to ask about his golf game.

Socializing is socializing; work is work. You should keep them separate, because you can be certain that the partners will.

There are two major behavioral rules that follow from this principle. First, be careful how you treat partners in the office. Do not get chummy. Lunch was lunch, but this is work. Do not park yourself in her office and initiate a lengthy discussion of the merits of Starbucks coffee. In fact, do not park yourself in her office at all.

This is not to say that friendships cannot be developed with senior attorneys—it is to say that you should not confuse business and pleasure. When in the office, the partner wants work to be done. When you are sitting in her office talking about office politics, that means that you are *not working,* and her blood pressure is rising by the minute. Work first, play later. Do not expect any special treatment because you are "friends." A round of golf does not make you friends. And even if it did, she would still expect the same performance from you in the office as she does from every other associate in the firm.

As a first-year associate, I found that I was very unhappy with the quality of work given to me by a particular partner. I thought it menial, tedious, and beneath me.

I voiced my concerns to another partner of the firm, with whom I felt I had established a good personal relationship.

This partner unceremoniously told me to stop my whining and complaining and just do the work. He also no doubt brought my complaining up at the next associate review session.

The second behavioral rule is the inverse of the first—be careful how you treat partners out of the office. Remember, when you are hanging out at the bar, trading some office gossip, that everything you say goes into the partner's memory banks, and may be brought up in gruesome detail during the next review session. The conversation may sound innocent to you, but everything you say can and will be used against you. So keep it light and friendly. This is not a good time to complain to partner X about the project you are doing for partner Y. Partner X and partner Y may have been friends for 30 years. This is a good time to discuss the merits of Starbucks coffee.

RULE NUMBER 15:

USE FIRM RESOURCES: THE LAW IS A TEAM SPORT

This rule is a variation of Rule #7—This is Not School; This is Not Homework. Law firms are completely goal-oriented. Where in school the purpose of the assignment is to teach you something, here the purpose is to accomplish the goal, preferably in the most efficient fashion possible.

As a result, we love plagiarism. Plagiarism 'R' Us. You will frequently encounter the phrase "don't reinvent the wheel." We want you to seek out the work of others. Before getting too deep into research, search the file system for memos on your subject. Start with someone else's work product instead of starting from scratch. Your firm will have a substantial collective memory— use it.

In fact, if you are drafting a document, particularly a contract, plagiarism is not only useful, it is actually required. The last thing anyone wants is a contract that you drafted from scratch. Always find a good "form"—a similar document from which you can start, and which provides "basic" language that you can modify. If you try to draft from scratch, you will at best have a contract written differently than every other contract out there (bad), and at worst omitting required provisions (far, far worse).

Remember too that when you find the memo that answers *exactly* your question, you cannot rely on it. Rule #3—Everything is Your Fault. You cannot simply put your name on that memo and hand it in. You must check and doublecheck and check again everything in it. Proofread, check the cites, check the law. If the memo is wrong (and therefore you are as well), it is not a valid excuse that the author of the memo is now a successful partner. Pre-existing work product is a starting point, never a finishing point.

Also use your support systems. Most large firms have in-house copy, fax, and scanning departments. Use them. Do not make your own copies, send your own faxes, or scan your own documents (except in an emergency)—that is wasteful. There are people whose job it is to do those things for you (but heed Rule #17). You have a secretary—take advantage of that. Many firms have significant library staff to help you with research, and perhaps even do cite checking and blue-booking for you. Learn about your firm's resources, and use them.

Another tremendous resource for you is your peers. Other associates or summer associates will know things that you do not, and will usually help you if they can (a corollary of which is that you should help others as well). Most firms have some sort of formal mentor program or advisor structure in place—use it.

There are, however, limitations. As a summer associate you are not authorized to delegate anything to another timekeeper (attorney or paralegal) without explicit authorization. The same almost certainly goes for junior associates, so learn your limitations.

And moreover—do not be lazy, and do not abdicate the project. The project was assigned to you, not to whomever you choose further down the line. Get help, but the project is still your job. Most importantly, when you delegate a part of the project, or get help with your copying, remember that Rule #3 still applies— Everything is Your Fault.

Rule Number 16:

Be Nice to Your Secretary

So it's the first day on the job, and you are (hopefully) being introduced around by another associate or recruiting person. As you approach your new office, the last stop is your secretary's desk. That's right, your secretary. You have a secretary. Now what?

Learning to work with a secretary takes some time. But there is one rule that should be the central guiding light in your dealings:

Be nice to your secretary.

This stands repeating: *Be nice to your secretary.*

Yes, having a secretary is new and exciting, and yes you are her boss (your secretary will still most likely be a woman). But it never ceases to amaze me how many

A mid-level associate, who had a rough relationship with her secretary, was in the middle of a closing. Everybody was scrambling to finalize all the documents by the funding deadline.

Unfortunately, one set of signature pages was not obtained in time, and the funding was delayed a day, to the great embarrassment of the associate, costing the client thousands of dollars.

The next day, the associate discovers the signature pages in a messenger envelope at her secretary's desk, where they had been since the day before.

When asked about the envelope, the secretary merely responded: "Oh, you needed those right away?"

junior associates, or even summer associates, think "secretary" is code for "sub-human slave."

Big mistake.

First, not being nice to your secretary is just rude. And pursuant to Rule #4—Be Socially Aware, you should be nice to everyone, not just your secretary. But you will, or at least could, have a closer working relationship with your secretary than just about anyone else in the office. She can help you in almost everything you do. You owe it to her to treat her well.

But, if human decency is not sufficient motivation, there are plenty of selfish reasons for treating your secretary well. As mentioned, you will see your secretary. A lot. A secretary can be your best ally, but also your worst enemy. If your secretary does not like you, you might find that there are more mistakes in your typing, your mailings go out a little later, your time sheets just missed the deadline, or a million other little things go wrong. And don't count on her volunteering to stay past 5 o'clock to help you out, either. Secretaries have broken the careers of many associates. They can break you. Do not become a statistic.

A secretary who likes you, however, can be the exact opposite. Do not cheat yourself of the opportunity to have the valuable asset: a good secretary. After a few months on the job, you will notice that some secretaries are much better than others. You will also notice that those secretaries are treated very well by their attorneys. This is not a coincidence.

To aggravate things, secretaries talk. Everything your secretary knows, all the other secretaries know.

Once you get a reputation, it will be difficult to get a better secretary, because you are now the demon boss. It does not matter how "justified" your behavior was—if your secretary does not like you, then you are the bad guy, and no secretary will volunteer to work for you again.

I once had a small disagreement with my secretary about how something should be done—the very next day another secretary came to my office to warn me that I was getting a reputation for being a tough boss.

So: Be nice to your secretary.

I mean, be really nice to your secretary. Say please and thank you. A lot. And buy her flowers for her birthday and for secretary's day. *This is important!* If you do nothing else right, make sure to get your secretary flowers (or chocolates, or some other suitable present) for her birthday and for secretary's day. Why? Because everybody else will, and secretaries talk.

This is one of the times when there is significant difference between a summer associate and a junior full-time associate. Both should be nice to their secretaries, but the relationship will by necessity be different. A junior associate is the secretary's boss. The associate may have to be delicate in establishing that relationship, and you should be a nice and gentle boss, but the associate is nevertheless the boss.

A summer associate, on the other hand, is nobody's boss. The secretaries know *exactly* where summer associates fit on the rank chart—they aren't on it. Summer associates are cute little children who come to play for a summer, and few secretaries will sit still for a summer associate who tries to boss her around. That's not quite right...very, *very* few secretaries will sit still for a summer associate who tries to boss her around. Remember that your secretary may have been with the firm for five, ten, twenty years or more—she is not impressed that you are in law school. She probably volunteered to help out the summer associates, so she probably has a good attitude, and she will try to help you. But *you are not her boss.* Make her your ally and your assistant, but remember that she works here—you are just interviewing. In fact, some firms ask secretaries to review the performance of summer associates.

So remember: Be Nice to Your Secretary.

An additional situation that warrants special mention is female attorneys and female summer associates. The overwhelming majority of secretaries in law firms today are women, and many attorneys are men. Many secretaries have worked for decades as secretaries, and only worked for men. Some went to secretary school decades ago, where they learned how to properly cross their legs and make good coffee.

This pattern is obviously changing year by year, as older secretaries retire and more women become attorneys. Nevertheless, many female associates and female summer associates will face problems dealing with secretaries. Many secretaries, consciously or otherwise, have greater difficulty accepting the authority of a 25-year-old woman than that of a man of the same age.

Is this right?

Wrong question. It does not matter whether it is right or not—it just *is*, and you have to deal with it. How? I do not have a good answer. I, of course, am a man, but my unscientific survey of female attorneys failed to reveal a universal solution to this problem. I can only recommend that you be aware of the situation, and employ Rule #4—Be Socially Aware. Watch closely how your secretary reacts to you, and adjust according-ly.

I have seen female attorneys successfully establish a more "chummy" relationship with their secretaries, and I have seen female attorneys successfully take a more distant "boss-like" approach. You will have to tailor your approach to your situation, and to your personality, but avoid either extreme (especially at first), and be sensi-tive to the additional challenges facing you. Be socially aware.

And be nice to your secretary.

RULE NUMBER 17:

HELP ANY WAY YOU CAN

So. You graduated from college, you graduated from law school. You have your framed diplomas hanging on the wall to prove it. You passed the bar exam, maybe even on the first try, and you are authorized to practice before the supreme court of your state. You are excited when the partner comes to your office to discuss your first big deal. And your assignment is...

Make some copies of the draft loan agreement. Bring the partner copies of some pages from a treatise. Order lunch. Proofread his secretary's typing.

What does he think you are? A copier, or a messenger, a food service worker, a clerical assistant?

Well, actually, yes he does. And he is right.

Yes, you are a highly educated professional. That's great. Now go get the copies.

It is a staggeringly common misconception, among summer associates and junior associates both, that this type of work is somehow "beneath" them. Well, you are all wrong. *Nothing* is beneath you. If you are a junior associate, you are the bottom of the food chain. If you

After a long day of negotiations for a major client on a large transaction, the CFO of the client had only one thing to say: "You didn't order my special sandwich."

This client had special dietary needs, and we had failed to meet them. The client was not happy, and neither was the partner.

are a summer associate, you are in training for the possibility to become the bottom of the food chain.

This is not hazing or some kind of strange initiation—it is simply work that must be done. Sometimes there is a training component to assignments, but lawyers do not get paid to do make-work. The best way to think of this, perhaps, is to ask yourself: "if not me, who?" I have a room full of clients, and my client wants coffee. Therefore, I send you to get coffee. Believe me, it will *not* make me happy if I have to get the coffee myself because you suddenly develop a superior attitude. The client wants coffee. Ergo there will be coffee. This request will be handled in exactly the same manner as if the client had requested a draft bill of sale, because, at that moment, it is just as important.

When I was a junior associate, the daily routine when there was a big deal underway was to prepare the FedEx distribution for the day. Significant amounts of documentation had to be copied, collated, and correctly organized for the various recipients. This could be a substantial undertaking, and we were continually pushing against the FedEx deadline. If it looked like we were in danger of missing the FedEx guy, the most junior person (me) would be dispatched to the mail room to "sit on" the FedEx guy, to ensure that he did not depart without our packages. The extent of my duties was not quite clear—I always wondered if I was expected to rassle the FedEx guy to the floor—but mostly I just stood in the mail room to make sure that the FedEx guy didn't leave. (Delivery people are usually on extremely tight schedules, so this is no small matter.)

And by the way, when you're getting that coffee, you had for your own sake better have a smile on your face. Seriously. This is not just about partners' reactions—although that's a huge part of it. You should be seriously, genuinely willing to help out, in absolutely any (legal) way possible. However, wherever, and whenever needed.

Highfalutin legal work? No. Essential to the success of the transaction? You bet.

Help in any way you can.

RULE NUMBER 18:

GREAT—YOU WERE A STUD IN SCHOOL. NOW SIT DOWN AND SHUT UP

Both summer associates and junior associates (and, sadly, many not-so-junior associates) suffer from a variety of insecurities. Perhaps this is not surprising, since a law office can be an intimidating place. Everywhere you turn, there are smart people, experienced people, people who (appear to) know what they are doing.

Many summer/junior associates react to this insecurity with a little innocent bragging. Some associates make sure that everyone in the room knows that they went to Harvard/Stanford/Chicago/Wherever, or that they were in the top 5% of the class, or that they aced the Bankruptcy exam, or that blah, blah, blah. This bragging, to a greater or lesser degree, is frightfully common.

Don't do it.

Just don't. Do not name-drop, do not grade-drop, do not LSAT-drop. Do not ask where everyone else went to law school. Nobody cares that you went to Harvard, and nobody cares about your GPA. That was interesting during recruiting interviews, but once you are hired, you are hired. The firm then *assumes* all that. While law firms operate on a strict hierarchy, they are at the same time, with some exceptions, remarkably egalitarian. The primary motivator for law firms is dollars. Unless your GPA allows the firm to raise your billing rate, the firm just does not care.

Remember, every lawyer at the firm was hired based on the same criteria. *Everyone there* is smart. They will not be impressed by your educational pedigree—they will only think you are obnoxious.

Don't be obnoxious.

Your whole life everyone has told you how much potential you have. You did well in high school, and they told you that you had great potential. You did well in college, and they told you that you had great potential. You did well in law school, and you told yourself that you had great potential. Well, it is time to convert that potential into results. Law firms do not care about potential. They care about results. Welcome to the real world.

Rule Number 19:

Carry a Pad—And Use It

This rule is near and dear to my heart. It also has two parts, and deals with form and substance.

Carry a pad, or a notebook, or *something* else to write on. Also, be sure to carry a pen to write with as well. Indeed, it's not a bad idea to have an extra pen attached to the pad.

Carry the pad and the pen everywhere. Everywhere. Bathroom, buddy's office, everywhere but lunch. Just walking out to the lobby to check the paper? Bring your pad. Running up to the library to grab a book? Bring your pad. Coming to my office? Make *sure* to bring a pad.

A partner at our firm, when she was a junior associate, was stopped by a senior partner on her way to the bathroom, without a pad. In passing, the partner asked her to draft up a "bullet" for him by the afternoon. Without anything to write on, she attempted to remember her task, but by the time she had left the bathroom the only thing she remembered was that it had something to do with guns. She spent the majority of the afternoon asking for help from senior associates trying to explain that she needed something about a gun.

Why is it so important to bring your pad every-where? Two reasons: First, you want to look like you are working. As a junior associate, there is virtually nothing within your job description that does not involve a writing pad. Therefore, if I see you without a pad in the hallway, I can only assume that you are not working. This is not a good thing for you. You will not get points for carrying a pad, but you will quickly lose them if you are seen, repeatedly, without one.

Second, you just might need it. Yes, hallway assign-ments do happen. Actually, they happen frequently. Do not be caught with your proverbial pants down.

This rule counts double if you are actually going to a partner's office. If you sit down in my office without a pen and a pad, you look lazy, arrogant, and unpre-pared—all at the same time!

This is not a good idea. Don't do it. Just bring the pad.

The second part of this rule is just as important. Few things are more aggravating than telling you all the per-tinent facts of the case and watching you *not* write them down. One of those few things is when you come crawl-ing into my office two hours later because you forgot something important that you did not write down. Another one of those things is when your document is all wrong because you forgot something important that you did not write down.

If I get sufficiently aggravated by your non-writing, I will specifically tell you to write something down. That is not a good sign. You are supposed to know, by instinct, osmosis, or otherwise, what to write down. If I have to tell you to write something down I will think less of you for it.

When in doubt, write it down.

So err on the side of writing down more rather than less. Be careful, however, not to overdo it! Also quite aggravating is watching you write down verbatim every word I say. Now I think you are not really listening and understanding, but just taking dictation, which is also not good.

Rule Number 20:

It's Your Career—It's Your Responsibility

Welcome to reality.

School is over. Regulated society is over. You are now a player in the capitalist marketplace, where it is every man for himself. There are no guarantees of success. There is injustice—sometimes a lot of it—and there are no appeals.

So watch out for number one. Protect Number One.

Some people mistakenly think that this principle means that you should climb over your friends and colleagues. Not true. In a good capitalist society, everyone benefits when you do what is truly best for yourself, and making other people hate you is not really a good idea. Creating enemies will almost certainly hurt. By definition, this is not good *for you.*

But this also means that you cannot count on others to take care of you. The coddling is now over. You will have mentors, advisors, support staff—all kinds of helpers. Most will genuinely try to help. But ultimately, it is your life, and your career. When something goes wrong (and it will!) it is *your* problem, not someone else's.

When the partner does not give you the deal he had promised you, and gives it to somebody else instead, there is no appeal. It is not fair, but it *is.* You have two choices: You can sit around moping (or worse, complaining) about it, or you can deal with the situation. I recommend the latter.

Bad things will happen to you, and not just on the job. But there are no make-up exams, no extra credit, and no do-overs. "It's not fair" is not a valid concern, or retort, any more. So stop your whining and complaining, and just *deal with it.*

Yes, nice people will try to help you. Yes, the firm will provide resources for you. But in the end, when it all comes down to it, it is your career, and that makes it your problem, your issue, and your responsibility.

What can you do about it? How do you protect Number One?

Learn.

The skills you acquire on your current job stay with you wherever you are. If you stay with the firm those skills will enhance your career at that firm. If you go elsewhere, those same skills will make that next job easier and better. (And don't think your former colleagues won't still play a role in your career. They will, sometimes for years to come.) Everyone wants the same thing—everyone wants you to become the best lawyer you can be, as fast as you can.

Do not wait for people to tell you to learn. Don't have enough work to fill the day? It will happen. You can either (a) play golf, or (b) read trade publications. Choice (a) is not necessarily a bad choice—golf skills can be valuable, and fun is after all allowed. But consider choice (b). You will acquire knowledge that will directly benefit the work that you will be doing tomorrow. It is not billable, so it does not "count" as work, but remember your goal—your overall goal is to enhance your legal career, not merely to bill hours. If (b) does not appeal to you, consider option (c)—do something else that is useful.

The partner gives you an asset purchase agreement, and asks you to review the indemnification clauses only. The partner says: "Don't read the whole contract; the ledger can't support another complete review." What should you do? Review the whole contract, of course. Is it billable? No. Will reading the whole agreement enhance your skills? Yes. So read it.

Your goal is to learn. Whenever you can, wherever you can. Do not wait for other people to tell you to learn.

Learn to learn for yourself.

Rule Number 21:

Just Do It!

An important feature of the practice of law is the surprising amount of workday discretion. There is no time clock, there is no assembly line, there are no surveillance cameras. You have a job to do, and it is up to you to make sure that it gets done.

As a result, procrastination is the great enemy. It is something we all face—even with a million demands on our time, we sometimes find a way not to do anything at all. Projects get pushed back, deadlines rushed. This only gets worse as you get more senior, when you are the one setting the deadlines. There is only one way to combat the evil of procrastination.

Just do it.

The only thing between a completed project and you is...you. You are your own greatest enemy, but you could be your own greatest ally.

Good luck.

About the Author

Morten Lund is a partner with the law firm of Foley & Lardner LLP, where he practices in energy and project finance. He attended Augustana College (the one in Rock Island) and Yale Law School. He lives in a quiet suburb of Milwaukee with his family, and has recently been taken in by the poker craze. He is a voracious reader of epic fantasy fiction, and has several works of his own in process, some of which may even be finished some day.

Index

OTHER LAW BOOKS
THE FINE PRINT PRESS

THE YOUNG LAWYER'S JUNGLE BOOK:
A SURVIVAL GUIDE, by Thane Messinger
ISBN 1-888960-19-1, 231 pages, US$18.95

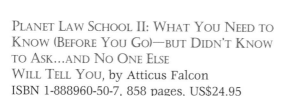

A career guide for summer associates, judicial clerks,
and all new attorneys. Advice on law office life,
including working with senior attorneys, legal research
and writing, memos, contract drafting, mistakes,
grammar, email, managing workload, timesheets,
annual reviews, teamwork, department, attitude,
perspective, working with clients (and dissatisfied
clients), working with office staff, using office tools, and yes, much more.

PLANET LAW SCHOOL II: WHAT YOU NEED TO
KNOW (BEFORE YOU GO)—BUT DIDN'T KNOW
TO ASK...AND NO ONE ELSE
WILL TELL YOU, by Atticus Falcon
ISBN 1-888960-50-7, 858 pages, US$24.95

An encyclopedic reference for each year of law
school. Examines hundreds of sources, and offers in-
depth advice on law courses, materials, methods,
study guides, professors, attitude, examsmanship,
law review, internships, research assistantships,
clubs, clinics, law jobs, dual degrees, advanced law
degrees, MBE, MPRE, bar review options, and the bar
exam. Sets out all that a law student must master to excel in law school.

LATER–IN–LIFE LAWYERS: TIPS FOR THE
NON–TRADITIONAL LAW STUDENT,
by Charles Cooper
ISBN 978-1-888960-06-8, 288 pages, US$18.95

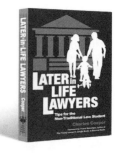

Law school is a scary place for any new student. For
an older ("non-traditional") student, it can be
intimidating as well as ill-designed for the needs of a
student with children, mortgages, and the like.
Includes advice on families and children; the LSAT,
GPAs, application process, and law school rankings
for non-traditional students; paying for law school; surviving first year; non-
academic hurdles; and the occasional skeleton in the non-traditional closet.